Are You The Universe?

Girish Bellalcheru - September 2024

Are You The Universe? by Girish Bellalcheru

First Printing Edition, 2024

This book is a work of non-fiction. While the author has made every effort to provide accurate information, the content is based on personal research, interpretations, and opinions. Readers should consult other sources when necessary. The publisher and the author disclaim any liability for any harm or damage that may result from the use or misuse of the information contained in this book.

For permissions, inquiries, or more information, contact:

StoneFeet Publishing

bookjabber@gmail.com

Disclaimer

The content of this book is intended for educational and informational purposes only. The author and publisher are not engaged in rendering professional advice or services, and the information in this book should not be considered a substitute for expert consultation in any related field, including but not limited to health, legal, or financial matters. Always seek professional advice when appropriate.

Table of Contents

Foreword

Part I

Are You the Universe?

The Echoes of the Universe

Chapter 1

The Sound of Creation

Chapter 2

Energy

Part II

Consciousness and the Cosmos

Chapter 3

The Emergence of Consciousness

Chapter 4

The Human Mind as a Resonator

Part III

The Quest for Human Potential

Chapter 5

The Drive to Understand Our Origins

Chapter 6

Reaching for the Highest Potential

Chapter 7

The Flow State

Part IV

The Next Evolution

Chapter 8

The Infinite Quest

Chapter 9

The end of an epic Journey

A Journey into the Resonance of Being

My journey into the resonance of being began in a unique environment where spirituality and science coexisted harmoniously. I was raised in a deeply spiritual and orthodox family that not only cherished traditions but also respected the discoveries of science. In our home, rituals were observed with reverence, and scientific curiosity was fostered with equal passion. This delicate balance between the spiritual and the scientific shaped my early worldview and ignited a lifelong quest to understand their deeper connections.

As I grew older, I couldn't help but notice the common threads that linked ancient traditions with modern science. Both paths, in their own ways, seemed to be pointing toward the same truths: that well-being, balance, and knowledge of the universe were integral to living a meaningful life. The spiritual practices I observed, meditation, prayer, and reverence for nature, aligned with the principles of science that governed the world around us. Yet, I found myself constantly questioning the commonality between these seemingly separate domains. What deeper truths bind them together?

Half my life has been dedicated to seeking answers, questioning, and trying to comprehend the confluence of spirituality and science. I've delved into the wisdom of ancient scriptures and philosophies, while also exploring the latest scientific research on the mind, consciousness, and the cosmos. This journey has been deeply personal and transformative, filled with moments of clarity and insight, as well as profound mysteries that still remain unsolved.

In recent years, as the internet has made an overwhelming wealth of research and material accessible, my understanding of the convergence between these paths has deepened. I realized that many of the ancient practices we have inherited are not just symbolic or ritualistic; they hold profound scientific truths about vibration, energy, and consciousness. I began to see how these timeless traditions were designed to align us with the rhythms of the universe, protect our well-being, and preserve an ancient knowledge that science is only now beginning to uncover.

It is with this understanding that I felt a deep need to share what I have learned with others. This book is a product of my journey, a journey that is not just mine but one that many of us are on. I believe that by exploring the resonance of being, this book will offer you new insights, inspiration, and perhaps even some answers to the questions you've been asking. More importantly, I hope it serves as a starting point for your own journey, one that might take you further than I have gone toward a deeper understanding of who we are and what we are all about.

In this book, you will explore the vibrations that form the foundation of the universe and our consciousness. From the ancient sound of Om to the latest scientific discoveries about energy flow, brainwaves, and collective consciousness, I hope to show you that these concepts are not as different as they seem. The journey toward self-actualization and beyond is a journey of harmonizing with the universe's vibrations and, in doing so, unlocking the highest potential within each of us.

Are You The Universe?

I invite you to walk with me on this path of exploration, where spiritual wisdom and scientific inquiry meet and where the search for meaning continues, always evolving and deepening.

Welcome to the journey.

Part I

Are You the Universe?

The Echoes of the Universe

Imagine the universe as a vast symphony, where every star, planet, and being plays its part in a never-ending vibration. The ancient sound of Om, believed to be the first sound of creation, echoes through the cosmos, shaping the very fabric of existence. Far from being merely mystical or spiritual, this sound symbolizes the fundamental forces that underpin reality. From quantum physics to spiritual traditions, vibrations are at the heart of everything we know.

In "Are You the Universe?", we embark on a journey to explore these cosmic echoes the vibrations that shape the stars, guide consciousness, and fuel our quest for meaning and self-actualization. This book connects the abstract idea of universal vibrations with our own existence, raising essential questions: What if we are in tune with these echoes? Could the patterns of the universe shape not only the physical world but also our minds, bodies, and potential?

A Journey from Sound to Self

For millennia, humans have searched for answers to life's biggest questions: Who are we? Where do we come from? What is our purpose? In this search, two paths have emerged—science and spirituality. Science seeks to understand the mechanics of the universe, from the Big Bang to quantum mechanics, while spirituality looks inward, exploring consciousness, meditation, and the soul's connection to the greater whole.

This book bridges these paths, suggesting that vibrations, the universe's underlying rhythm, may hold the key to understanding both our origins and our potential. From the vibrations of atoms to the resonance of sound in meditation, these universal rhythms connect everything, from the smallest particle to the grandest star.

The Search for Meaning and Potential

What does it mean to be in sync with the universe? Could tuning into these echoes unlock our hidden potential? Throughout history, many have believed that tapping into these vibrations can lead to deeper awareness, greater creativity, and even extraordinary abilities heightened intuition, healing, or wisdom.

The Call to Tune In

Through science, spirituality, and the quest for personal growth, "Are You the Universe?" asks: What if we're not just observers of the cosmos but active participants in its symphony? What if aligning ourselves with the universe's vibrations is the key to unlocking who we truly are? This book invites you to listen closely to the echoes around and within you, to consider the possibility that the universe is speaking and perhaps, in some way, you are it.

Chapter 1

The Sound of Creation

The universe began not with silence but with a vibration. For millennia, spiritual traditions have echoed this idea none more prominently than the ancient concept of Om, often described as the primordial sound of creation. But what if this mystical sound, revered by sages and seekers, is not just symbolic? What if it points to something fundamental about reality, resonating through spiritual teachings and modern science?

This chapter explores the idea that vibration is the foundation of all existence, a concept that spans ancient wisdom and cutting-edge physics. From the Big Bang to the subtle energy fields within our bodies, vibrations shape the universe and perhaps even our consciousness.

The Mystical Om: More Than a Sound

Om has been chanted for millennia, a sacred syllable believed to embody the essence of the cosmos. It is more than a word it's an experience, a vibration that aligns the mind, body, and spirit with the universe.

In Hinduism, Om is the sound of the universe's birth, symbolizing existence's infinite, eternal, and unchanging essence. When chanted, Om is not just heard; it's felt, resonating within the body and calming the mind, as if it tunes us into the frequency of the universe itself.

Ancient texts like the Upanishads suggest that Om is the sound from which all matter originates. According to these teachings, chanting Om connects us to the vibrations that created the stars, planets, and life. While this may sound poetic, modern science is now uncovering the reality behind this metaphor.

One of the most profound descriptions of Om and its significance in creation can be found in the Mandukya Upanishad, which is dedicated entirely to exploring Om as the fundamental sound of the universe. The Upanishad explains the nature of reality and consciousness through the symbol and sound of Om, emphasizing that it encompasses everything—past, present, future, and beyond.

The Mandukya Upanishad begins with this famous verse:

"Om ity etad akṣaram idaṃ sarvam, tasyopavyākhyānaṃ bhūtaṃ bhavad bhaviṣyad iti sarvam oṅkāra eva"

Translation: "Om, the imperishable sound, is all this. It explains that which was, is, and will be—indeed, everything is Om."

This verse from the Mandukya Upanishad encapsulates the essence of Om. It emphasizes that Om is not just a sound but the primordial vibration from which the universe originates. In Hindu cosmology, Om represents the eternal and formless Brahman, the ultimate reality that permeates everything. It is both the seed sound of creation and the soundless reality beyond creation.

The Science of Sound and Vibration

The universe, a grand symphony of vibrations, is not silent. Despite the apparent vacuum of space, modern science unveils a cosmic orchestra, where waves of energy vibrations are fundamental to the structure and evolution of the universe.

Physicists have long known that everything, from atoms to galaxies, vibrates at specific frequencies. String theory, a prominent theory in modern physics, suggests that the most fundamental particles of the universe are not tiny solid objects but vibrating strings of energy. These vibrations give rise to different particles and forces, much like the strings of a violin produce different notes. String theory suggests that everything in the universe is connected through tiny, vibrating strings, and understanding these vibrations could help us unlock the mysteries of how the universe works at the most significant and smallest scales.

In this view, the universe is a cosmic symphony, with each particle vibrating at a unique frequency, creating its complexity. This concept resembles the ancient idea of Om, the sound from which all creation emerges. Could Om symbolize the universal vibrations that shape reality?

Even in the vacuum of space, where sound as we know it cannot travel, vibrations exist in the form of electromagnetic and gravitational waves, reverberating through the cosmos and influencing matter.

The "Music of the Spheres"

Ancient cultures, like the Greeks, believed the universe emitted a "music of the spheres," a cosmic harmony resulting from the movements of celestial bodies. This idea, developed by Pythagoras, suggests that the ratios governing musical harmony also govern the orbits and relationships of planets. For Pythagoras and his followers, the universe was interconnected through mathematics, with music as a tangible expression of cosmic order.

This concept of cosmic harmony, resonating through the universe, is not just a philosophical idea. It finds its echo in modern physics, which suggests that everything in the universe is in motion, vibrating at various frequencies. This interconnectedness, this harmony, is what binds us to the cosmos, making us feel a part of something greater.

Recording the "Sound" of the Universe

While traditional sound cannot travel through space, scientists have captured cosmic vibrations that can be translated into sound-like data. One example is the Cosmic Microwave Background (CMB), the "afterglow" of the Big Bang, representing the echo of the universe's birth. NASA's WMAP and Planck satellites have mapped these fluctuations, translating them into deep, reverberating hums that suggest the early universe was far from silent.

Another groundbreaking discovery came in 2015: LIGO's detection of gravitational waves. These waves, ripples in spacetime caused by massive cosmic events, like the collision of black holes, were converted into audible frequencies, a quick rising tone or "chirp" that allowed us to "hear" the universe's most cataclysmic events.

Similarly, NASA's Chandra X-ray Observatory captured the low-frequency sound waves emitted by a supermassive black hole in the Perseus galaxy cluster, demonstrating that even the farthest reaches of space resonate with vibrations.

Cymatics: Sound Shapes Reality

In the modern world, the study of cymatics shows us the tangible effects of sound on matter. By observing how particles like sand or water droplets organize themselves in response to sound frequencies, we see that sound has the power to create order out of chaos.

German physicist Ernst Chladni demonstrated this by using sound to produce geometric patterns in sand, known as Chladni figures. Swiss scientist Hans Jenny expanded on this, visualizing sound's impact on various substances and suggesting that vibration shapes reality at a fundamental level.

These experiments suggest that sound and vibration play a central role in structuring matter, much like the cosmic vibrations that give rise to the universe. This idea aligns with ancient philosophies, such as the Music of the Spheres and the concept of Om.

Order from Chaos: The Resonance of the Universe

One of the most intriguing aspects of vibration is its ability to bring order from chaos. Both spiritually and scientifically, vibrations are seen as the organizing principle that turns random energy into structured forms.

In a spiritual sense, Om represents the transition from the unmanifested to the manifested, from pure potential to creation. Scientifically, vibrations, whether they are the oscillations of particles or waves of sound, give rise to the structure of reality.

This is mirrored in resonance, where one object vibrating at a specific frequency causes another to vibrate at the same frequency. Resonance may hold the key to understanding how different parts of the universe are connected in a grand, interconnected web of vibrations.

The Significance of Om in Indian Tradition

In Vedic philosophy, Om is considered the first sound that emerged from the cosmic void during creation. The Mandukya Upanishad explains that Om encompasses all states of consciousness, such as waking, dreaming, deep sleep, and a transcendental state (Turiya). This makes Om a sound that can transcend the physical and reach the metaphysical.

Chanting Om, a central practice in yoga and meditation for thousands of years, is not just a ritual. It is a transformative experience believed to balance energies and bring practitioners closer to their inner selves. The silence that follows the chant is equally significant, symbolizing transcendence and pure consciousness, inspiring us to delve deeper into our spiritual journey.

The Universe as a Symphony

In this chapter, we have explored the idea that the universe is built on vibrations, from the spiritual concept of Om to modern theories like string theory and cymatics. These vibrations are not just abstract; they are a tangible force that shapes the cosmos and our consciousness.

As we move forward, we will continue to explore how these vibrations define the universe and guide our quest for meaning and potential. The sound of creation still echoes through the cosmos, and by tuning in, we might discover how to resonate with it.

References:

1. The Upanishads by Eknath Easwaran (ISBN: 978-1586380212)

2. The Principal Upanishads by S. Radhakrishnan (ISBN: 978-8172231248).

3. The Elegant Universe by Brian Greene (ISBN: 978-0393338102). This book introduces string theory, which proposes that the universe's fundamental building blocks are tiny, vibrating strings.

4. Parallel Worlds by Michio Kaku (ISBN: 978-1400033720) explores multiverses and string theory

5. First Year Wilkinson Microwave Anisotropy Probe (WMAP) Observations: Preliminary Maps and Basic Results (Astrophysical Journal Supplement Series, 2003).

6. The Harmony of the Spheres: A Sourcebook of the Pythagorean Tradition in Music by Joscelyn Godwin (ISBN: 978-0892812656).

7. Schumann Resonance and its Effect on Human Behavior published in the International Journal of Environmental Research and Public Health (2018).

Chapter 2

Energy

At the most fundamental level, reality is composed of energy. While solid objects like the chair you're sitting on seem stable, modern physics reveals that everything is in constant motion. The atoms and subatomic particles that makeup matter vibrate at incredible speeds.

Quantum mechanics, which explores the behavior of particles at the smallest scales, reveals a universe in perpetual motion. Electrons, for instance, don't orbit the nucleus in fixed paths but exist in a cloud of probabilities, constantly vibrating.

One of the most striking theories in modern physics, string theory, suggests that the smallest units of matter aren't particles but tiny, vibrating strings of energy. These strings vibrate at different frequencies, forming everything from electrons to photons. The entire universe is a network of vibrations, with various forms of matter and energy as varying expressions of these underlying frequencies.

The Resonance of Life: Biological Vibrations

Vibrations aren't confined to the subatomic level. Our bodies are vibrational systems, too, from the beating of the heart to the firing of neurons. Every organ, cell, and molecule vibrates at its own frequency, creating a complex, interconnected web of energy.

Traditional healing systems like Ayurveda and Chinese medicine recognize the importance of vibrations in the body. These systems are based on the flow of life force prana or qi through energy channels. When this energy becomes stagnant, illness arises. Chakras, or energy centers, are said to vibrate at specific frequencies, and imbalance in these vibrations can affect physical, emotional, and spiritual health.

In Ayurveda, prana is considered the vital life force that permeates the body and mind and governs all physical, emotional, and spiritual functions. It is the energy that flows through all living beings, sustaining life and playing a central role in maintaining health and well-being. The concept of prana is closely linked to breath, energy channels, and the balance of the body's internal systems.

The word prana comes from the Sanskrit roots "pra" (before) and "an" (to breathe or live), meaning "that which sustains life." Prana is more than just breath—it represents the subtle energy that animates all living beings. This energy flows through nadis (energy channels) and is concentrated in the body's chakras (energy centers).

Ayurveda identifies five subdivisions of prana, called the Pancha Vayu (five winds), each governing different bodily functions. Prana Vayu, located primarily in the head, chest, and throat, governs the inhalation of breath, intake of sensory impressions, and higher mental functions such as creativity, focus, and perception. Apana Vayu, located in the lower abdomen and pelvis, governs elimination processes, including urination, defecation, menstruation, and childbirth. Samana Vayu, centered in the stomach and small intestine, is responsible for digestion and the absorption of nutrients. It creates equilibrium and balances prana and apana. Udana Vayu, located in the throat and head, governs speech, expression, and upward movements like belching or vomiting. It also facilitates spiritual growth and higher states of consciousness. Vyana Vayu pervades the entire body and manages circulation, muscle movement, and coordination. It helps distribute prana throughout the body and connects all other vayus.

Prana flows through an intricate network of nadis, or subtle energy channels, within the body. There are 72,000 nadis, among which the Ida Nadi, Pingala Nadi, and Sushumna Nadi are the most significant. When prana flows freely and the chakras are balanced, health, vitality, and well-being exist. If the flow of prana is blocked, it can lead to physical, emotional, and spiritual imbalances.

Ayurveda recommends practices such as pranayama (breath control) and yoga asanas (postures) to restore prana flow and maintain balance. These practices regulate prana flow and clear energy blockages.

The Body's Electromagnetic Field

Modern research reveals that the human body generates its own electromagnetic fields. Measurable by an ECG, the heart's field is the most powerful, extending several feet beyond the body. The brain produces its own waves, which can be tracked by EEG. Brain states like relaxation and creativity correspond to different frequencies.

Emerging evidence even suggests that humans may possess some degree of magnetoreception, the ability to sense magnetic fields, though this is much more developed in animals like birds. This suggests our bodies might be more attuned to the Earth's electromagnetic field and cosmic forces than we realize.

The Power of Resonance: Tuning into the Universe

At the heart of vibration is resonance, the phenomenon where one object vibrating at a specific frequency causes another object to vibrate in sympathy. Resonance doesn't just apply to musical instruments; it has profound implications for how we interact with the world around us.

Our thoughts, emotions, and consciousness also vibrate at different frequencies. Positive emotions like peace and love raise our vibration, positively influencing ourselves and others, while negative emotions like fear and anger lower it, creating disharmony.

Resonance is at the core of practices like meditation, yoga, and mindfulness. These practices aim to elevate our internal vibrations, aligning us with the natural rhythms of the universe and allowing us to tap into a deeper connection with cosmic vibrations.

The Chakra System: Pathways of Energy Flow

In Indian spiritual traditions, particularly yoga and Ayurveda, the body contains seven main chakras, or energy centers, aligned along the spine. Each chakra governs different physical, emotional, and spiritual aspects of life, vibrating at its own frequency:

1. Root Chakra (Muladhara) – Grounding and survival, located at the base of the spine.

2. Sacral Chakra (Svadhisthana) – Creativity and emotion, located just below the navel.

3. Solar Plexus Chakra (Manipura) – Personal power and self-esteem, located in the stomach.

4. Heart Chakra (Anahata) – Love and compassion at the center of the chest.

5. Throat Chakra (Vishuddha) – Communication and truth, located at the throat.

6. Third Eye Chakra (Ajna) – Intuition and insight, located between the eyebrows.

7. Crown Chakra (Sahasrara) – Spiritual connection and enlightenment, located at the top of the head.

When these chakras are in harmony, energy (prana) flows freely through the body, promoting health and well-being. Practices like chakra meditation and energy healing aim to restore this balance, allowing us to align our bodies with cosmic energies.

Scientific Explorations into Energy and Health

Modern science is beginning to explore how subtle energy fields influence health. The HeartMath Institute has shown that the heart's electromagnetic field can synchronize with the brain's, promoting coherence between the two, which leads to emotional and cognitive benefits. This research shows that heart coherence, where the heart and brain operate in sync, is a state of optimal health and efficiency.

Are You The Universe?

Biofield science explores the energy fields surrounding living beings, suggesting they play a crucial role in maintaining physical, emotional, and spiritual health. While controversial, researchers like Dr. William Tiller have conducted experiments suggesting that human intention can influence physical matter, providing a possible link between mind-body interactions and healing.

Balancing Earth Energies and Sacred Geometry

Ancient Indian traditions emphasized aligning the body's energy with cosmic forces. Sacred spaces, such as temples, were often built with sacred geometry, designed to resonate with the Earth's energy and promote spiritual alignment.

This concept of energy alignment is reflected in geopathic stress zones, areas where the Earth's magnetic field may disrupt human health. Ancient builders sought to create spaces that fostered harmony between humans and the cosmos by using geometry and understanding Earth's energies.

Temples were often constructed according to sacred geometry, emphasizing the use of proportions and shapes believed to resonate with natural energies. This geometric precision was thought to create a resonance between the temple structure and the Earth, thereby neutralizing or avoiding any potential negative energy from the environment. Evidence suggests that ancient builders used techniques to detect energetic disturbances in the ground, such as water veins or magnetic fields. By identifying geopathic stress points, they could place critical parts of the temple (such as the sanctum or the main deity) in energetically optimal spots.

Yantras (geometric diagrams representing divine forces) and sacred symbols were often embedded in temple foundations.

These yantras were believed to serve as energy conduits, attracting positive vibrations and dispelling negative ones. Even today, in some Indian temple construction practices, geopathic stress is considered through modern vastu principles and earth energy testing. The ancient Indian understanding of geopathic stress, though not termed as such, was deeply integrated into their spiritual and architectural practices. Temples were viewed as buildings and sacred spaces designed to harmonize human existence with cosmic and terrestrial energies.

In Vastu Shastra, the Vastu Purusha Mandala is the cosmic geometric design or grid used in planning and building a temple or any other structure. In Sanskrit, the term Purusha is derived from the root "puru" meaning "to cover" or "to envelop," suggesting a being that encompasses or pervades the entire universe. These ancient practices of balancing Earth's energies resonate with modern concepts of geopathic stress and how they highlight humanity's long-standing awareness of the unseen forces that influence our lives.

Vibration as the Key to Reality

Vibration is the foundation of reality, whether in quantum mechanics, biological systems, or spiritual practices. It connects everything from subatomic particles to cosmic waves, and understanding these vibrations could unlock the mysteries of existence.

By recognizing ourselves as participants in this vibrational reality, we open the door to living in greater harmony with the universe. As we attune ourselves to the rhythms of the universe, we begin to see that vibrations are not just the building blocks of matter but of consciousness itself. The more we align with these frequencies, the more we can unlock our potential, heal, and find deeper connections with the world around us.

Everything Vibrates, Everything Connects

This chapter has explored how vibrations are the fundamental building blocks of reality. From quantum physics to ancient traditions, the concept of vibration permeates every level of existence.

As we continue this journey, we will explore how these vibrations influence consciousness and how understanding them might help us achieve our highest potential. Everything vibrates, and everything is connected. By attuning ourselves to these cosmic frequencies, we may discover our deeper place in the universe.

References:
1. Quantum Mechanics: The Theoretical Minimum by Leonard Susskind and Art Friedman (ISBN: 978-0465062904)

2. The Fabric of the Cosmos by Brian Greene (ISBN: 978-0375727207)

3. The Elegant Universe: Superstrings, Hidden Dimensions, and the Quest for the Ultimate Theory by Brian Greene (ISBN: 978-0393338102)

4. Cymatics: A Study of Wave Phenomena and Vibration by Hans Jenny (ISBN: 978-1888138078)

5. Handbook of Atmospheric Electrodynamics edited by Hans Volland (ISBN: 978-0849353220)

6. The Body Electric: Electromagnetism and the Foundation of Life by Robert O. Becker and Gary Selden (ISBN: 978-0688069711)

7. The Sevenfold Journey: Reclaiming Mind, Body, and Spirit Through the Chakras by Anodea Judith and Selene Vega (ISBN: 978-0895945740)

8. Energy Medicine: The Scientific Basis by James L. Oschman (ISBN: 978-0443062612)

9. The Tao of Physics: An Exploration of the Parallels Between Modern Physics and Eastern Mysticism by Fritjof Capra (ISBN: 978-1590308356)

10. Vibrational Medicine: The #1 Handbook of Subtle-Energy Therapies by Richard Gerber (ISBN: 978-1879181588)

Part II

Consciousness and the Cosmos

Part II

Consciousness and the Cosmos

As we explored in Part I, the universe is a vast symphony of vibrations, with everything from the tiniest particles to the grandest galaxies vibrating in harmony. But there is one vibration that remains a mystery, consciousness. How does consciousness arise in a universe governed by energy and vibrations? And could it be that our awareness, thoughts, and sense of self are inextricably linked to the same forces that shape the cosmos?

In Part II: Consciousness and the Cosmos, we turn our attention inward, exploring the profound connection between the mind and the universe. For centuries, humans have grappled with the question of consciousness, what it is, where it comes from, and whether it's unique to living beings or a fundamental aspect of reality itself. As we dig deeper into this age-old mystery, we'll consider whether consciousness is not just a byproduct of complex biology but rather an inherent property of the universe, woven into the very fabric of space and time.

Consciousness: A Cosmic Phenomenon?

Could it be that consciousness is more than just an individual experience—that it is, in fact, a universal force, vibrating in harmony with the cosmos? Ancient spiritual traditions have long suggested that consciousness is connected to something far greater than the individual self. In Hindu philosophy, for example, Atman (the self) is seen as inseparable from Brahman (the ultimate reality), suggesting that our awareness is but a reflection of the cosmic mind.

In modern scientific thought, consciousness remains one of the most elusive phenomena. Neuroscientists have made strides in understanding how the brain processes information, but the nature of subjective experience the "hard problem" of consciousness remains largely unsolved. Could the key to unlocking this mystery lie in the vibrations we've been exploring? Some researchers propose that consciousness may arise from the quantum level, from the very vibrations that form the foundation of reality.

A Bridge Between Science and Spirit

In this section, we'll explore the fascinating intersection between spiritual insights into consciousness and scientific inquiries into the nature of the mind. From meditation and mindfulness practices that raise awareness to quantum theories that suggest consciousness may permeate the universe, we'll seek to bridge the gap between the metaphysical and the measurable.

We'll delve into how practices like meditation, which aim to align our internal vibrations with higher frequencies, can lead to altered states of consciousness, greater self-awareness, and even a sense of oneness with the cosmos. Are these experiences merely subjective, or do they point to a deeper truth about the nature of consciousness and its connection to the universe?

Consciousness as a Key to Potential

Are You The Universe?

Ultimately, this section is about more than just understanding consciousness—it's about how this understanding can help us reach our highest potential. Throughout history, many have believed that tapping into higher states of consciousness can unlock extraordinary abilities, from heightened intuition to enhanced creativity and wisdom. But beyond individual growth, there's a bigger question: What role does consciousness play in the evolution of humanity?

As we journey through Part II: Consciousness and the Cosmos, we'll explore whether consciousness is not only the key to our individual potential but also a driving force in the universe's own evolution. Could it be that the universe itself is becoming more self-aware, with human consciousness acting as one of the many instruments in this cosmic awakening?

The Cosmic Mind: Where Science Meets Spirituality

As we embark on this exploration of consciousness, we will ask profound questions that challenge the boundaries of both science and spirituality:

- Is consciousness a universal phenomenon, present throughout the cosmos?

- Could our minds be in tune with the vibrations of the universe, creating a deeper connection between us and everything around us?

- And how can this understanding help us live more fulfilling, purpose-driven lives?

In this part of the journey, we'll examine the echoes of consciousness that reverberate throughout the universe, and explore how aligning ourselves with these cosmic vibrations can lead to profound self-realization.

Chapter 3

The Emergence of Consciousness

As we've seen, the universe is a breathtakingly intricate network of vibrations, energies, and patterns. From this cosmic dance, one of the greatest mysteries arises consciousness. How does awareness emerge from the seemingly mechanical processes of the universe? And why does it exist at all? In this chapter, we delve into the origins of consciousness from the dawn of life to its complex evolution in humans, pondering whether consciousness is not an accident but an inevitable outcome of the universe's underlying laws.

The Origins of Life and Consciousness

Life on Earth began billions of years ago, likely as simple molecules that formed the first self-replicating organisms through random interactions and environmental conditions. But how did this lead to awareness of the ability to perceive, think, and feel? Many theories attempt to explain the emergence of consciousness, ranging from purely biological to deeply metaphysical.

The human brain, the most complex structure in the known universe, is composed of billions of neurons interacting in intricate webs of electrical and chemical signals. This organ did not appear overnight; it is the result of millions of years of evolutionary refinement. Over time, early human ancestors developed larger and more complex brains, leading to advanced traits like language, abstract thinking, and self-awareness.

Consciousness is often described as an emergent property, a phenomenon that arises from the interactions of simpler components, in this case, the brain's neural networks. The interaction of billions of neurons gives rise to subjective experiences, thoughts, and emotional phenomena that cannot be fully explained by studying individual neurons in isolation.

At the heart of this mystery is the question: Is consciousness a product of complex biological systems, or does it represent a deeper, intrinsic aspect of the universe? Some researchers suggest that the same physical principles governing forces like gravity and quantum mechanics might also explain the emergence of consciousness.

Consciousness: An Inevitable Outcome?

One compelling theory posits that consciousness was inevitable, a natural consequence of the universe's tendency toward complexity and self-organization. The same physical laws that formed galaxies and stars could also lead to living organisms capable of processing information, culminating in brains capable of conscious thought.

As the universe evolved, matter organized itself in increasingly complex ways, forming molecules, cells, and eventually brains sophisticated enough to generate what we call consciousness, a self-aware system capable of introspection, creativity, and abstract thinking.

From this perspective, consciousness is not an isolated phenomenon but a natural extension of the universe's evolution. Life, intelligence, and awareness are seen as progressions in a universe striving toward greater complexity, coherence, and order. In this sense, we are the universe becoming aware of itself, with consciousness as a universal property that arises under the right conditions.

Is Intelligence Just Mathematics?

Is intelligence simply an expression of mathematics, a way the universe encodes and processes information? Intelligence, whether human or artificial, involves recognizing patterns and solving problems based on rules and logical structures. Some scientists and philosophers suggest that intelligence might be a form of universal pattern recognition, an emergent property of how information flows through the universe.

The universe can be seen as a vast informational network where patterns of energy and matter interact according to mathematical laws. Intelligence, whether in human brains or computer algorithms, maybe the natural expression of these laws, allowing the universe to optimize its complexity and organization.

This idea suggests that intelligence is not unique to humans but is an inherent property of the universe's structure, allowing the cosmos to process and understand itself through complex beings like us.

The Role of Consciousness in the Universe

If consciousness and intelligence arise from the universe's laws, what role does consciousness play in the cosmic scheme? Some interpretations of quantum mechanics suggest that consciousness may directly influence reality. The famous observer effect proposes that the act of observation impacts quantum events, raising the question of whether consciousness is fundamental to the nature of existence.

The anthropic principle argues that the universe must have properties that allow conscious beings to exist because otherwise, we wouldn't be here to observe it. This has led some to speculate that consciousness is not just a byproduct of the universe but a necessary feature intertwined with its evolution.

Another intriguing concept is panpsychism, which is the belief that consciousness is a fundamental aspect of all matter, not just living beings. According to this view, every particle in the universe has some form of consciousness, which evolves into higher forms as matter becomes more complex, eventually giving rise to human awareness.

The Multiverse and Consciousness

The multiverse theory suggests that our universe may be just one of countless others, each with unique physical laws. In some universes, conditions may never allow life and consciousness to arise, while in others like ours, the specific arrangement of forces enables the evolution of conscious beings.

In this view, the multiverse acts as a cosmic laboratory where countless combinations of physical laws play out, producing a wide range of realities. Our universe is one of the rare "successful experiments" where the conditions are just right for life and consciousness to emerge.

This perspective suggests that consciousness is not merely a local phenomenon but part of a much larger, multiverse-wide process. Consciousness in our universe may be a byproduct of fine-tuned constants, such as the strength of gravity or the charge of electrons, that allow life to evolve over billions of years.

Why Did Consciousness Evolve?

Why did consciousness evolve at all? One hypothesis is that consciousness provides an adaptive advantage, allowing organisms to process information, make decisions, and plan for the future. In humans, consciousness has enabled the development of language, culture, and technology, contributing to our success as a species.

Yet, consciousness comes with a cost. Self-awareness brings the knowledge of mortality and the capacity for existential anxiety. However, this very awareness drives humans to seek meaning and strive for self-actualization.

The Fine-Tuning Problem and the Anthropic Principle

Our universe appears to be fine-tuned for life. If certain physical constants were slightly different, life as we know it wouldn't exist. For example, if the force of gravity were stronger, stars might burn out too quickly for life to evolve. The anthropic principle offers an explanation: we observe the universe as fine-tuned because we exist in one of the universes where conditions were right for consciousness to emerge.

Consciousness as the Essence of Existence

The Upanishads, ancient Indian scriptures that form the philosophical core of Hinduism, offer profound insights into the nature of consciousness. They explore consciousness as the ultimate reality that underlies and sustains all existence. In the Upanishadic worldview, consciousness is not confined to individual minds but is the universal essence—the fundamental reality that pervades everything, often referred to as Brahman. The Upanishads also emphasize the intimate connection between the individual soul (Atman) and this universal consciousness.

Brihadaranyaka Upanishad (1.4.10): "अहं ब्रह्मास्मि" (Aham Brahmasmi)

Translation: "I am Brahman."

This is one of the most famous Upanishadic declarations, emphasizing that the true self (Atman) is identical to Brahman, the universal consciousness. It conveys the idea that individual consciousness is not separate from the ultimate reality but is a reflection or manifestation of it.

Mundaka Upanishad (2.2.9): "द्वा सुपर्णा सयुजा सखाया समानं वृक्षं परिषस्वजाते । तयोरन्यः पिप्पलं स्वाद्वत्त्यनश्नन्नन्यो अभिचाकशीति ॥"

Translation: "Two birds, inseparable companions, perch on the same tree. One eats the fruit, the other looks on."

This metaphor symbolizes the relationship between the individual self (Atman) and the witnessing consciousness (Brahman). One bird (the individual soul) is engrossed in the material world, while the other bird (Brahman) silently witnesses without attachment. It illustrates how true consciousness is ever-present, observing the individual experiences but remaining unaffected by them.

In the Upanishads, consciousness is both the universe's source and substance. It transcends physical reality and yet permeates every aspect of existence. Realizing the oneness of Atman and Brahman is the key to spiritual enlightenment, a state in which one understands that consciousness is the underlying truth of the cosmos.

One of the central tenets of the Upanishads is the identification of Atman (the inner self or individual consciousness) with Brahman (the universal consciousness). The Upanishads teach that the true self of every individual is not the body or mind but the Atman, which is eternal, infinite, and identical to Brahman. Realizing this unity is considered the ultimate goal of life, leading to liberation (moksha).

The Cosmic Puzzle: Intelligence, Life, and Meaning

As we delve deeper into the origins of consciousness, it becomes clear that intelligence, life, and the cosmos are interconnected in ways we are only beginning to understand. Is the universe itself intelligent, evolving toward greater awareness through conscious beings like us?

Whether consciousness is an inevitable byproduct of cosmic laws or a fundamental feature of the universe, one thing is certain: it is the key to unlocking our understanding of reality. Our ability to reflect on the cosmos and ask profound questions is a testament to the power of conscious thought.

In this chapter, we've explored how consciousness might have emerged from the universe's laws and whether it plays a critical role in shaping reality. As we continue our journey, we will explore how consciousness connects us to the cosmos and whether it may be the very essence of the universe itself.

References:

1. The Upanishads by Eknath Easwaran (ISBN: 978-1586380212)

2. The Principal Upanishads by S. Radhakrishnan (ISBN: 978-8172231248)

3. A Simple Introduction by Pravrajika Vrajaprana (ISBN: 978-0970636804)

4. Galileo's Error: Foundations for a New Science of Consciousness by Philip Goff (ISBN: 978-1524747961)

5. The Conscious Mind: In Search of a Fundamental Theory by David Chalmers (ISBN: 978-0195117899)

6. The Feeling of Life Itself: Why Consciousness Is Widespread but Can't Be Computed by Christof Koch (ISBN: 978-0262039307)

7. Mandukya Upanishad with Gaudapada's Karika by Swami Nikhilananda (ISBN: 978-8175050167)

8. Quantum Enigma: Physics Encounters Consciousness by Bruce Rosenblum and Fred Kuttner (ISBN: 978-0195144086)

9. The Archetypes and the Collective Unconscious by Carl G. Jung (ISBN: 978-0691018331)

10. Tao Te Ching by Lao Tzu (Translated by Stephen Mitchell, ISBN: 978-0061142666)

Chapter 4

The Human Mind as a Resonator

The human brain, a remarkable organ, processes information through oscillatory activity, where neural networks fire in rhythmic patterns. These brainwaves, spanning a spectrum from delta to gamma frequencies, are each associated with different states of consciousness, such as sleep, relaxation, focused thought, or heightened awareness. This rhythmic activity, a reflection of the vibrational patterns observed across nature, from atomic to cosmic scales, underscores the brain's role as a resonator. It is capable of syncing its internal rhythms with external influences, from sound waves to cosmic forces, demonstrating its adaptability and its profound connection to the universe.

In this chapter, we delve into the intriguing possibility that resonance might influence perception and cognition. Could certain frequencies amplify specific thoughts or emotional states, similar to how an instrument resonates more powerfully when aligned with its natural frequency? This leads us to a profound question: could our thoughts, emotions, and even consciousness be an expression of the brain's potential to tune into the vibrational frequencies of the universe, highlighting its remarkable ability to perceive and interact with its environment?

The Brainwave Spectrum

Brainwaves are typically classified into five main categories, each corresponding to different mental states.

Delta Waves (0.5 – 4 Hz) are associated with deep, dreamless sleep and unconsciousness. They are the slowest brainwaves and are primarily present during the stages of deep sleep, which is crucial for physical restoration, healing, and growth. Theta Waves (4 – 8 Hz) are associated with light sleep, meditation, creativity, and emotional processing. They are also linked to memory retrieval and creativity. Studies show theta waves increase during mindfulness meditation, enabling greater access to emotional regulation and deep introspection.

Alpha Waves (8 – 12 Hz) are associated with relaxation, calm focus, and wakeful rest. Studies demonstrate that alpha waves increase when individuals close their eyes or relax and decrease when people engage in tasks requiring focused attention. Beta Waves (12 – 30 Hz) are associated with alertness, active thinking, problem-solving, and focused attention. Beta waves are linked to cognitive tasks, and studies using EEGs have demonstrated that beta waves increase during activities requiring sustained attention and problem-solving. Gamma Waves (30 – 100 Hz) are associated with higher states of consciousness, heightened awareness, peak focus, and cognitive processing. Gamma waves are linked to the "binding problem" in neuroscience, how the brain integrates disparate sensory inputs into a unified experience. Research has found elevated gamma activity during states of heightened focus and in individuals practicing advanced meditation, indicating deeper levels of consciousness.

Over the past few decades, neuroscience has increasingly focused on understanding how these oscillatory brain patterns relate to different states of consciousness. In a well-known study by Richard Davidson and colleagues (2004), EEGs were used to measure brainwaves of Tibetan monks engaged in deep meditation (loving-kindness meditation). The study found a significant increase in gamma wave activity, particularly in long-term practitioners, suggesting heightened levels of awareness and synaptic synchronization. This study demonstrates that advanced meditation can enhance gamma wave activity, which is associated with heightened awareness and compassion. The synchronization of brain regions during these gamma waves suggests a higher level of brain coherence.

A 2013 study by Mölle and Born examined the relationship between theta activity and creative problem-solving. They found that theta waves increased during creative tasks and were particularly active during moments of insight. This research showed that theta waves facilitate creativity and intuition, reinforcing that brainwaves reflect mental activity and the brain's ability to tap into deeper cognitive processes.

Some researchers suggest that human brainwaves may synchronize with the Schumann Resonance, leading to a state of natural coherence between the brain's frequencies and the Earth's electromagnetic fields. Studies in biofield science suggest that exposure to natural environments and reduced exposure to artificial electromagnetic fields can increase alpha brainwave activity, improving mental clarity and well-being.

The Mirror of Nature's Rhythm

The rhythmic activity of brainwaves mirrors the vibrational patterns observed across nature. The alignment between brainwave patterns and natural vibrations suggests that human consciousness might be inherently connected to the rhythms of the universe. Just as the Earth resonates at a specific frequency, so does the human brain, indicating a possible resonance between cosmic and biological systems. The fact that brainwaves oscillate in predictable patterns across different states of consciousness aligns with the broader idea that vibration and frequency underlie the structure of both the mind and the cosmos.

Meditation, Chanting, and Synchronizing with Vibrations

Ancient spiritual practices like meditation and chanting have long recognized the power of sound and rhythm to influence consciousness. Chanting mantras like "Om" produces vibrations that are believed to align the mind with the universe's fundamental frequency, underscoring the power of these practices in helping individuals connect with the cosmos.

Meditation is widely recognized as a practice that can bring about profound changes in brain function and consciousness. One of the key effects of meditation is the synchronization of neural activity, which refers to the harmonious coordination of different brain regions. This synchronization can enhance mental clarity, emotional regulation, and cognitive efficiency. Scientific research has increasingly shown that meditation, through its influence on brainwave activity, leads to measurable changes in the brain that reflect a more coherent and balanced mental state.

Meditation quiets the mind and allows it to enter more synchronized states of consciousness. During deep meditation, brain activity shifts into slower, more coherent rhythms, such as theta waves, which are often linked to introspective awareness and heightened intuition. This enlightening process suggests that these practices may help the mind tune into subtle vibrational energies, facilitating a deeper connection between the individual and the cosmos.

Scientific research on meditation has shown that it can alter brainwave activity, increasing coherence and synchronization across different regions of the brain. This provides a neurological framework for understanding how ancient practices create measurable shifts in brain function, supporting the idea that such techniques help the brain resonate more effectively with its environment.

In a study conducted by J. E. Cahn and J. Polich (2006), experienced meditation practitioners showed a significant increase in alpha-wave activity during meditation. This increase was particularly pronounced in mindfulness meditation, where participants were trained to focus on the present moment without judgment. The researchers found that this enhanced alpha activity was correlated with reduced stress, emotional stability, and greater mental clarity. Meditation-induced alpha waves are believed to promote a sense of inner calm and centeredness, helping practitioners achieve a synchronized state of mind where thoughts are less scattered.

Key studies have found that meditation can increase coherence across alpha, theta, and gamma waves, linked to states of inner peace, creativity, and focused attention.

Neuroscience and Ancient Wisdom

Modern neuroscience is increasingly interested in the connection between brainwaves and states of consciousness. Studies have shown how neural entrainment, where external rhythms, such as sound or light, synchronize with brainwaves, can influence cognitive states. For instance, listening to rhythmic drumming or repetitive chanting may induce entrainment, aligning brain activity with external frequencies and creating a sense of oneness or transcendence.

Meditation not only synchronizes brainwaves but can also lead to structural changes in the brain. Neuroplasticity, the brain's ability to reorganize itself, is enhanced through regular meditation. A study by Sara Lazar et al. (2005) used MRI scans to examine the brains of long-term meditation practitioners. They found that regions of the brain associated with attention, emotional regulation, and self-awareness (such as the prefrontal cortex and hippocampus) showed increased gray matter density in those who meditated regularly. The study suggests that meditation leads to long-term brain changes that improve cognitive functioning, emotional regulation, and the brain's ability to integrate sensory and emotional information. This enhanced brain plasticity supports the idea that meditation not only synchronizes brain activity but also enhances the brain's capacity for learning, growth, and self-awareness.

Ancient wisdom traditions such as yoga, Tibetan Buddhism, and Indian metaphysical philosophy have long explored these connections, using practices that aim to align individuals with cosmic energies. The potential of modern neuroscience to validate these insights is intriguing, suggesting that these ancient practices may have tapped into universal principles of resonance and vibration that underlie the brain's function and the structure of the universe.

The Brain as a Cosmic Tuning Fork

This chapter delves into the awe-inspiring possibility that the human brain, through its natural rhythms and the power of resonance, may act as a tuning fork for the universe. Practices like meditation and chanting could serve as ways of attuning our minds to the cosmic vibrations that shape reality. As neuroscience continues to explore these connections, we may uncover a deeper understanding of the brain's role as both a resonator and a receiver of the universe's frequencies, hinting at a profound unity between consciousness and the cosmos.

References
1. Cahn, B. R., & Polich, J. (2006). Meditation states and traits: EEG, ERP, and neuroimaging studies. Psychological Bulletin, 132(2), 180–211.

2. Lutz, A., Greischar, L. L., Rawlings, N. B., Ricard, M., & Davidson, R. J. (2004). Long-term meditators self-induce high-amplitude gamma synchrony during mental practice. Proceedings of the National Academy of Sciences, 101(46), 16369–16373.

3. McCraty, R., Atkinson, M., & Bradley, R. T. (2009). Electrophysiological evidence of intuition: Part 1. The surprising role of the heart. Journal of Alternative and Complementary Medicine, 15(4), 393–400.

4. Dietrich, A. (2004). Neurocognitive mechanisms underlying the experience of flow. Consciousness and Cognition, 13(4), 746–761.

5. Baer, R. A. (2003). Mindfulness training as a clinical intervention: A conceptual and empirical review. Clinical Psychology: Science and Practice, 10(2), 125–143.

6. Sheldrake, R. (2009). The Science Delusion: Freeing the Spirit of Enquiry. ISBN: 978-1444727930

7. Bohm, D. (1980). Wholeness and the Implicate Order. ISBN: 978-0415289795

8. Davidson, R. J., & McEwen, B. S. (2012). Social influences on neuroplasticity: Stress and interventions to promote well-being. Nature Neuroscience, 15(5), 689–695.

9. Lazar, S. W., Kerr, C. E., Wasserman, R. H., Gray, J. R., Greve, D. N., Treadway, M. T., McGarvey, M., Quinn, B. T., Dusek, J. A., Benson, H., Rauch, S. L., Moore, C. I., & Fischl, B. (2005). Meditation experience is associated with increased cortical thickness. NeuroReport, 16(17), 1893–1897.

10. Konig, H. L., & Ankermüller, F. (1979). Earth's Electrical Environment. ISBN: 978-0309031816

11. Goff, P. (2019). Galileo's Error: Foundations for a New Science of Consciousness. ISBN: 978-1524747961

Part III

The Quest for Human Potential

Part III

The Quest for Human Potential

Humanity's pursuit of its highest potential has shaped civilizations, inspired philosophies, and driven technological progress. But what compels us to continuously seek to transcend our current state? Whether through spiritual enlightenment, scientific breakthroughs, or personal growth, humans have always strived to unlock new dimensions of existence.

In this section, we explore the boundless drive for self-mastery—from ancient practices aimed at achieving higher consciousness to modern innovations that push the limits of human abilities. This quest raises fundamental questions: What are we striving for? Is there an ultimate goal, or is the pursuit of potential itself the essence of human existence?

Through this exploration, we look at how spiritual wisdom and scientific discovery intersect, revealing how ancient traditions like meditation, energy work, and mind-body practices are now being validated by cutting-edge research. From the mysteries of human consciousness to the power of cognitive and physical enhancements, this part delves into the many facets of unlocking human potential. It also invites us to consider the ethical, philosophical, and existential implications of the paths we are taking.

Ultimately, this section guides us to reflect on whether true potential lies in expanding outward—through technology and physical mastery—or turning inward, seeking deeper understanding and unity with the universe. The quest for human potential may be the most important journey of all, and it defines the future trajectory of our species.

Chapter 5

The Drive to Understand Our Origins

Since the dawn of civilization, humans have sought answers to fundamental questions about our origins: Where do we come from? Why are we here? How did the universe begin? This relentless curiosity is deeply tied to our nature as conscious beings. The drive to understand our origins is intertwined with the human quest for meaning, self-awareness, and purpose. This chapter explores how humanity's deep-seated curiosity about the origins of life and the cosmos connects to our evolution as conscious beings and why this pursuit is central to understanding who we are.

The Ancient Quest for Origins

Throughout history, cultures worldwide have created origin stories and narratives that explain the creation of the universe, life, and humanity. From ancient Mesopotamian myths to the cosmogonies of Egypt, Greece, and India, these stories attempted to make sense of the mysteries of existence.

Many of these myths depict the universe as arising from Chaos or a primordial state. In Greek mythology, Chaos precedes the ordered universe, while in Hinduism, creation emerges from a cosmic ocean of potentiality driven by sound, specifically Om, which represents the essence of creation.

These stories share a common thread: they provide a narrative framework that allows humans to place themselves within a larger cosmic story. This suggests that the quest for origins is not merely intellectual but rooted in a deep-seated human need to understand our place in the universe.

In classical philosophy, thinkers like Aristotle and Plato pondered the nature of existence and the origins of the cosmos. Aristotle's concept of the prime mover posited an unmoved force responsible for the initial motion of the universe. At the same time, Plato's theory of the Forms suggested that the physical world reflects a higher, ideal reality that transcends time and space.

The drive to understand our origins is often tied to the quest for meaning. As self-aware beings, we seek to reconcile our finite existence with the infinite, shaping both our philosophical and scientific endeavors.

Brahman as the Source of Creation

The Upanishads describe Brahman as the ultimate, formless, and unchanging reality that is the source of everything. From Brahman, the universe and all living beings emanate. Brahman is both transcendent and immanent, meaning it exists beyond the physical universe but also pervades all of creation.

सदेव सोम्य इदमग्र आसीदेकमेवाद्वितीयम्।

Transliteration: Sadeva somya idamagra āsīdekamevādvitīyam.

Translation: "In the beginning, my dear, this world was just Being, one only without a second."

This passage reflects the idea that all life, including human beings, originated from a single source: the eternal and undifferentiated Being. Everything that exists is a manifestation of this primordial reality.

According to the Upanishads, Atman, the individual self, is identical with Brahman. The realization of this unity is the ultimate goal of human existence. Therefore, humans' origins are linked to their essential nature as divine beings, emanations of Brahman. This cosmic connection implies that all humans are not separate entities but united in the same spiritual essence.

Mundaka Upanishad (2.1.10): "As the spider weaves its web out of itself, and as small sparks fly from the fire, so from the imperishable, all things here have come."

The Upanishad uses the metaphor of a spider weaving a web to describe how all beings, including humans, emerge from Brahman as sparks emerge from a fire. Just as sparks are not separate from the fire, humans are not separate from Brahman.

Scientific Perspectives: The Origins of Life and the Universe

Scientific advances in the 20th century provided new insights into the universe's origins. The Big Bang theory describes the universe's beginning as an infinitely dense point that rapidly expanded around 13.8 billion years ago, leading to the formation of galaxies, stars, and planets.

Yet, fundamental questions remain: What existed before the Big Bang? Was the universe created from nothing, or is it part of an eternal cycle of creation and destruction? These questions continue to fuel scientific inquiry, driven by the same existential curiosity that has animated human thought for millennia.

The Origins of Life

The question of how life began on Earth is another key focus of both philosophical and scientific inquiry. The theory of abiogenesis suggests that life arose from non-living matter through chemical processes. At the same time, the panspermia hypothesis proposes that life may have originated elsewhere in the cosmos and traveled to Earth via comets or asteroids.

Recent discoveries of extremophiles, organisms that thrive in extreme conditions, have led scientists to reconsider the potential for life beyond Earth, perhaps in the subsurface oceans of Europa (a moon of Jupiter) or even in the clouds of Venus. These investigations echo the same curiosity that inspired mythological and philosophical reflections on life's origins.

The Quest for Meaning

At the heart of human existence is the desire to find meaning. This drive is often tied to the question of origins; where we come from is closely linked to why we are here. Unlike other animals, humans are not content merely to exist; we seek to understand our purpose in the grand scheme of the cosmos.

Existential philosophers like Jean-Paul Sartre and Albert Camus have reflected on this drive for meaning, often concluding that it is an inherent part of the human condition. According to Camus, life's meaning may not be given to us but is something we create through our actions and choices.

Consciousness and Self-Awareness

Consciousness plays a central role in our desire to understand our origins. Unlike other creatures, humans possess a heightened sense of self-awareness, allowing us to contemplate our existence in relation to the vastness of the universe. This capacity to reflect on our own thoughts, origins, and place in the cosmos has driven many of humanity's greatest intellectual and spiritual achievements.

The quest for self-awareness is also connected to the idea of self-actualization. As conscious beings, we not only seek to understand where we come from but also strive to understand who we are and what we are capable of. This leads to an exploration of our potential, both as individuals and as a species.

The Search for Cosmic Connection

Many spiritual traditions suggest that understanding our origins is not just about uncovering the past but also about realizing our connection to the universe. Indigenous worldviews often emphasize the interconnectedness of all living things, while

Are You The Universe?

Hindu philosophy presents Brahman as the ultimate reality underlying the universe, of which we are all an integral part.

Some modern theories, like panpsychism, propose that consciousness itself may be a fundamental aspect of the universe. According to panpsychism, consciousness exists in all matter, from the smallest particles to the largest structures, suggesting that the universe may be aware of itself in some way.

Transcending Individual Awareness

As our understanding of the universe expands, so too does our sense of cosmic awareness. Just as individuals seek to understand their personal origins, humanity as a whole is on a journey toward understanding its collective origins in the cosmos.

This drive toward cosmic awareness may lead to a new stage in human evolution, where our understanding of the universe expands to include a spiritual dimension. Philosopher Pierre Teilhard de Chardin envisioned this as the Omega Point, where humanity's collective consciousness converges toward a higher state of awareness, bringing us closer to understanding both the universe and ourselves.

The drive to understand our origins is not simply about uncovering the past. It is about answering the deepest questions arising from our conscious awareness: Who are we? Where do we come from? What is our purpose? This quest is central to human nature and is reflected in every aspect of our history, from mythology and philosophy to science and spirituality.

As we continue to explore the mysteries of the cosmos, we also explore the nature of our consciousness and potential. The search for origins is, in many ways, a search for self-understanding, and through this pursuit, we may come to realize the true depths of what it means to be human.

References
1. Deamer, D. (2011). First Life: Discovering the Connections between Stars, Cells, and How Life Began. University of California Press.

2. Camus, A. (1942). The Myth of Sisyphus. Gallimard.

3. Radhakrishnan, S. (1953). The Principal Upanishads. Harper & Row.

4. Greene, B. (2004). The Fabric of the Cosmos: Space, Time, and the Texture of Reality. Vintage Books.

Chapter 6

Reaching for the Highest Potential

Humans have always aspired to reach their highest potential, seeking growth across physical, emotional, intellectual, and spiritual dimensions. This chapter explores the journey of self-actualization through both psychological and spiritual lenses, examining how practices like yoga, meditation, and scientific inquiry provide pathways for individuals to realize their fullest capabilities.

Additionally, we explore how vibrations, energy, and consciousness shape our understanding of personal growth, revealing how ancient wisdom and modern science intersect in the pursuit of higher self-awareness and potential.

Maslow's Theory of Self-Actualization

Maslow's Hierarchy of Needs is a psychological theory that explains how human beings move through different levels of needs in their lives, starting from basic survival needs to reach their highest potential. It's often shown as a pyramid with five levels, and a person needs to fulfill the needs at the lower levels before moving to the higher ones. The first level at the pyramid's base includes the most basic things we need to survive: food, water, air, sleep, and warmth. Without these, it's hard to focus on anything else. A person who is hungry or thirsty will think only about getting food or water. These are the essentials for staying alive.

The first level at the pyramid's base includes the most essential things we need to survive: food, water, air, sleep, and warmth. Without these, it's hard to focus on anything else. A person who is hungry or thirsty will think only about getting food or water. These are the essentials for staying alive. Once the person feels physically safe, they seek relationships, friendship, love, and a sense of belonging. Humans are social creatures, and at this level, they want to feel connected to others, whether through family, friends, or a romantic partner. Next is the Esteem Needs level, where people seek respect, recognition, and self-esteem. They want to feel good about themselves and gain the respect of others. This includes self-confidence and a sense of accomplishment. People at this stage want to be seen as competent and valued in what they do, which could involve work achievements, personal successes, or community involvement.

Abraham Maslow introduced the concept of self-actualization as the highest level of human psychological development. This is about becoming the best version of yourself and reaching your full potential. It means using your talents, pursuing your passions, and achieving personal goals that give you a deep sense of purpose and fulfillment. People at this stage are driven by personal growth and creativity, not by the need for approval or rewards. They are curious, open to learning, and continuously growing.

At the top of this hierarchy is self-actualization, the point at which individuals fully realize their potential. For Maslow, self-actualized people are creative, autonomous, and driven by intrinsic values such as personal growth, compassion, and justice rather than external rewards. They pursue meaningful goals like artistic expression, community service, or scientific discovery, live authentically, and are motivated by personal growth.

Maslow later expanded his theory to include self-transcendence, the idea that individuals who reach self-actualization may seek to connect with a higher purpose beyond their personal identity. This suggests that human potential is not confined to the individual but is part of a greater cosmic or collective potential.

People don't always move up the pyramid in a straight line. Life can cause shifts—if you lose your job, for instance, you might focus again on safety needs. But generally, as each level of need is fulfilled, you can focus on higher needs.

To reach self-actualization, a person must first have their basic needs met (food, shelter), feel secure and safe, have meaningful relationships, and feel respected and confident. Once these are in place, they can start focusing on personal growth, creativity, and realizing their full potential.

In simple terms, it's about moving from surviving to thriving and ultimately becoming the person you are truly capable of being.

The Spiritual Perspective

In spiritual traditions, self-actualization is closely linked to achieving higher states of consciousness. Practices like yoga and meditation aim to elevate the mind, body, and spirit, leading to a deeper understanding of one's true nature.

Yoga integrates physical postures (asanas), breath control (pranayama), and meditation (dhyana) to achieve balance and harmony. Through these practices, the mind becomes focused and attuned to the body, facilitating greater self-awareness.

Meditation, particularly mindfulness and concentration practices, help individuals transcend ego-driven thoughts and experience a state of pure awareness. This shift allows for self-actualization as individuals become more attuned to their inner nature and purpose.

In many spiritual traditions, self-realization refers to recognizing the divine or eternal self beyond the limitations of the body and ego. This realization is the ultimate goal of understanding that one's true nature is interconnected with the universe. In Vedanta philosophy, for instance, self-realization involves recognizing the Atman (individual soul) as identical with Brahman (universal consciousness).

Yoga and the Path to Self-Actualization

Yoga is more than a physical practice; it is a comprehensive system for achieving balance and self-mastery. Through asanas, pranayama, and meditation, yoga empowers individuals to align their body and mind with the universal flow of energy, enabling them to achieve mental clarity and emotional balance.

Yoga philosophy teaches that the mind and body are intimately connected. Through disciplined practice, one can attain higher states of awareness and even reach Samadhi, a state of union with the divine or the universe. This path leads practitioners toward self-actualization by cultivating inner peace and harmony with the world.

Raja Yoga

Raja Yoga, also known as the "royal path" of yoga, focuses on mastering the mind and achieving spiritual growth through meditation and discipline.

Swamy Vivekananda explains the eight limbs of yoga (Ashtanga Yoga), which include Yama (ethical disciplines), Niyama (self-purification and study), Asana (posture), Pranayama (breath control), Pratyahara (withdrawal of the senses), Dharana (concentration), Dhyana (meditation) and Samadhi (union with the divine)

Vivekananda introduces Raja Yoga as a method for controlling the mind and achieving union with the higher self (Atman). He explains that through Raja Yoga, individuals can reach a state of self-mastery, transcending the mind and body's limitations. A major focus of Raja-Yoga is learning how to control the mind through meditation and concentration. He emphasizes the importance of Dharana (concentration) and dhyana (meditation) in stilling the mind and transcending the ego, allowing individuals to experience the pure consciousness that leads to spiritual awakening.

Vivekananda stresses that yoga is not just a religious practice but a science of the mind. He explains that through disciplined practice and experimentation, individuals can observe the effects of yoga on their mental and spiritual well-being. He encourages a rational, empirical approach to understanding spirituality. The ultimate aim of Raja Yoga is to achieve Samadhi, a state of spiritual absorption where the individual soul (Atman) merges with the universal consciousness (Brahman).

Meditation and Consciousness

Meditation has long been recognized as a practice for expanding consciousness and facilitating personal growth. By quieting the mind and focusing attention, meditation allows individuals to access deeper levels of awareness, unlocking their full potential.

Various forms of meditation, such as mindfulness, transcendental meditation, and Vipassana, enable practitioners to explore their thoughts, emotions, and consciousness. Through this exploration, individuals gain insight into their true selves and the interconnectedness of life, fostering self-actualization.

Meditation is also linked to neuroplasticity, the brain's ability to reorganize itself. Studies show that regular meditation can increase gray matter density in areas related to learning, memory, and emotional regulation, suggesting that consciousness itself can evolve through dedicated practice.

Science and Human Potential

While spiritual practices are often associated with self-actualization, the pursuit of scientific knowledge is also a path toward human potential. Scientists seek to understand the workings of the universe, from the smallest subatomic particles to the largest cosmic structures, driven by the same quest for truth and meaning that underlies spiritual exploration.

Scientific inquiry fosters curiosity, creativity, and a deep sense of wonder about the nature of existence. By exploring the laws of physics, biology, and cosmology, science not only expands human knowledge but also helps individuals tap into their intellectual and innovative potential, driving humanity forward.

The idea that the universe is made of vibrations and that everything resonates at a particular frequency has profound implications for personal growth. By aligning with higher vibrations, whether through sound, movement, or mental focus, individuals can raise their own vibrational frequency, fostering positive transformation.

Energetic Alignment and Personal Growth

Energetic alignment plays a crucial role in personal growth. When individuals are in tune with their own inner vibrations and the frequencies of their environment, they experience balance, harmony, and clarity. This alignment allows for a more fluid expression of creativity, intuition, and purpose key elements in achieving one's highest potential.

Self-Actualization and Cosmic Connection

Whether approached through psychology, spirituality, or science, the journey toward self-actualization is a quest to reach our highest potential. Maslow's hierarchy, Eastern practices, and modern scientific insights all point to the same underlying truth: humans are capable of extraordinary growth and transformation.

By engaging in practices that cultivate awareness, balance, and vibrational alignment, we can transcend our limitations and unlock the full range of our potential. Ultimately, self-actualization is not just a personal achievement but a realization of our connection to the broader universe, recognizing that we are both creators and participants in the ongoing evolution of life and consciousness.

References
1. Maslow, A. H. (1943). "A Theory of Human Motivation." Psychological Review, 50(4), 370-396.

2. Vivekananda, S. (1980). Raja-Yoga. Advaita Ashrama.

3. Yogananda, P. (1946). Autobiography of a Yogi. Self-Realization Fellowship

4. Iyengar, B. K. S. (1966). Light on Yoga: Yoga Dipika. Schocken Books.

5. Davidson, R. J., & Begley, S. (2012). The Emotional Life of Your Brain: How Its Unique Patterns Affect the Way You Think, Feel, and Live—and How You Can Change Them. Hudson Street Press.

6. Motoyama, H. (1981). Theories of the Chakras: Bridge to Higher Consciousness. Theosophical Publishing House.

7. Maslow, A. H. (1969). The Farther Reaches of Human Nature. Viking Press.

8. Csikszentmihalyi, M. (1990). Flow: The Psychology of Optimal Experience. Harper & Row.

Chapter 7

The Flow State

The term Flow, popularized by psychologist Mihaly Csikszentmihalyi, offers a deep understanding of individuals intensely engaged in their passions. Whether it's an artist painting or an athlete competing, the flow state is characterized by complete absorption in the task, a sense of timelessness, and effortless concentration. Understanding and achieving Flow is a significant intellectual achievement, representing one of the highest expressions of human potential. This understanding can be applied in various fields, from sports to creative arts and everyday tasks, to enhance performance and well-being.

The Role of Energy in Achieving Flow

To enter the flow state, both the mind and body need to be in sync, with energy flowing freely throughout the system. This connection to ancient Indian wisdom, which suggests that this free Flow of energy allows us to access higher states of consciousness and efficiency, begs the question of whether many of the ancient practices were a journey to lead us to the peak of human potential.

Breath Control and Energy Flow

Scientific studies of pranayama (breath control), which regulates energy flow throughout the body, show that deep rhythmic breathing synchronizes the brain's activity with the heart's electromagnetic field, a process known as heart-brain coherence. When the breath is steady, the brain produces alpha waves associated with calm focus and relaxation. This brain coherence enhances creativity, problem-solving, and the ability to stay in Flow.

Chakra Alignment and Flow

According to ancient Indian wisdom, when the chakras, the body's energy centers, are aligned, prana flows smoothly through them, fostering a harmonious relationship between the body and mind. This alignment can make us feel more balanced and focused, contributing to the mental clarity, emotional stability, and heightened focus necessary to achieve Flow.

The Brain in Flow

Modern research into electromagnetic fields and brainwave states offers a scientific understanding of how the body and mind enter Flow. Brainwaves, the rhythmic electrical activity of the brain, come in different patterns, each linked to various mental states, ranging from deep sleep to high alertness. Flow is closely associated with the alpha (8-12 Hz) and theta (4-8 Hz) brainwave states, which are linked to relaxed concentration, creativity, and intuition.

Research shows that individuals in Flow often exhibit alpha-theta brainwave coherence, where these frequencies are harmonized.

Are You The Universe?

This state enables heightened focus, deep learning, and creative insights. Practices like chakra meditation and sound therapy can help induce this brainwave coherence, making it easier to access Flow.

Flow, Heart Coherence, and Physical Performance

Studies from the HeartMath Institute show that during Flow, the heart's electromagnetic field becomes more coherent and synchronizes with brain activity. This synchronization, measurable through ECGs and EEGs, enhances mental focus and physical performance. In athletes, Flow often corresponds with moments of peak physical performance, where the body operates in harmony without conscious effort.

Meditation and the Flow State

Meditation practices, especially those involving sound vibrations or chakra alignment, are often used to train the mind to enter Flow more easily.

Chanting a mantra like Om brings the mind into deep concentration, aligning energy flow with the body's natural rhythms. This state of inner calm is a precursor to flow, quieting mental chatter and allowing for sustained focus. Studies show that chanting mantras induces theta brainwave activity, which is linked to creative problem-solving and intuition, which are key aspects of Flow. Mindfulness meditation encourages being fully present, helping individuals stay engaged in tasks with greater ease and Flow.

The Role of the Environment in Inducing Flow

Energy flow and electromagnetic fields are influenced by external environments. Several factors can support or disrupt the energy flow necessary for achieving Flow. Understanding and optimizing these factors in our surroundings can significantly contribute to our ability to enter and sustain the flow state.

The Schumann Resonance, the Earth's natural electromagnetic frequency, is around 7.83 Hz and synchronizes with the brain's alpha waves. Like natural landscapes, exposure to environments with strong Schumann Resonance promotes mental clarity and Flow. Conversely, urban environments with high levels of artificial electromagnetic fields, such as those from electronic devices like smartphones and Wi-Fi routers, may disrupt the body's natural balance, hindering Flow.

The Science of Flow and Health

Flow not only enhances performance but also improves mental and physical health. Research at Claremont Graduate University shows that individuals who regularly experience Flow exhibit higher levels of neuroplasticity, enhancing learning and adaptability. Flow increases the release of dopamine and norepinephrine, boosting focus, motivation, and emotional resilience. Another study in Psychological Review found that people in flow show improved immune function and reduced levels of cortisol (the stress hormone), suggesting that Flow supports both mental performance and overall health. This holistic understanding of Flow can inspire us to strive for this state for performance and our well-being.

Research published in Consciousness and Cognition shows that during Flow, the brain experiences enhanced synchronization across different regions. This leads to transient hypofrontality, a temporary reduction in activity in the prefrontal cortex (responsible for self-monitoring and doubt), allowing individuals to act without second-guessing, a hallmark of the flow state. This concept is crucial to understanding how the brain functions in the flow state.

Flow as the Pinnacle of Human Potential

The Flow state represents the pinnacle of human potential, where energy, focus, and action are seamlessly integrated. Ancient practices like chakra alignment, meditation, and sound healing help regulate the body's energy flow and align it with larger cosmic rhythms, such as the Earth's natural electromagnetic frequency, making it easier to access Flow.

In this chapter, we've explored how the electromagnetic fields of the heart and brain play a central role in Flow and how aligning these fields through meditation, breathing practices, and a harmonious environment can promote sustained focus and creativity.

References
1. Csikszentmihalyi, M. (1990). Flow: The Psychology of Optimal Experience. Harper & Row.

2. Austin, J. H. (1998). Zen and the Brain: Toward an Understanding of Meditation and Consciousness. MIT Press.

3. Sudarshan Kriya Yogic Breathing in the Treatment of Stress, Anxiety, and Depression: Part I—Neurophysiologic Model." Journal of Alternative and Complementary Medicine

4. Bradley, R. T., & McCraty, R. (2015). "The Influence of Cardiac Coherence on State Anxiety and Emotional Regulation." Frontiers in Psychology

5. Tang, Y. Y., Hölzel, B. K., & Posner, M. I. (2015). "The Neuroscience of Mindfulness Meditation." Nature Reviews Neuroscience

Part IV

The Next Evolution

Part IV

The Next Evolution

As humanity approaches the peak of its potential, the question arises: What comes next? In this part, we explore the profound transformations awaiting us after self-actualization, whether through the lens of transhumanism, spiritual enlightenment, or the emergence of a collective consciousness.

Is human growth finite, or will it continue into new dimensions of existence? With advancements in technology, science, and spirituality, we could unlock extraordinary abilities within ourselves—abilities that ancient traditions have long spoken of but modern science is just beginning to explore. This section invites you to consider whether humanity's next evolution will be driven by the power of the mind or through radical enhancements of our physical and cognitive capacities.

Could unlocking heightened consciousness lead to the discovery of extraordinary abilities? This chapter delves into the ancient claims of superpowers such as intuition, telepathy, and heightened spiritual insight. These abilities, which have been described in esoteric traditions, are now being explored through the lens of modern neuroscience and scientific research.

Part IV

Chapter 8

The Infinite Quest

Many spiritual traditions suggest that self-actualization is merely the beginning of a deeper journey. Once we reach our highest potential, the focus naturally shifts from personal growth to contributing to a larger purpose. This transition brings a profound sense of fulfillment, as we use our wisdom, skills, and abilities to help others reach their potential or selflessly serve humanity.

Those who achieve personal mastery often feel compelled to leave a positive legacy through creative contributions, social change, or helping solve global issues like environmental sustainability, equality, or justice. Some suggest that the next step is to contribute to the collective evolution of consciousness, helping others elevate their awareness and fostering a more harmonious world.

A Journey Beyond Self

Transcendence is often seen as the next stage after self-actualization. Psychologist Abraham Maslow, who introduced the concept of self-actualization, later added another stage: self-transcendence. In this stage, individuals go beyond personal achievements, seeking to connect with something more significant, such as spiritual enlightenment, cosmic awareness, or connection to universal consciousness and a deep understanding of the interconnectedness of all life.

In this transcendent state, personal goals align with a greater purpose, contributing to the collective well-being. This supports the idea that human potential has no definitive peak, and there's always more to explore, enhance, and contribute.

In fact, for self-actualized individuals, personal goals are often in sync with the greater good. Their pursuit of a career or passion fulfills them and positively impacts the world. Creativity is a hallmark of this stage, as individuals express their highest potential in ways that enhance the world around them.

A New Quest for Understanding

Self-actualization may lead to a new quest, one of exploration and deepening understanding. Just as science continually evolves, each discovery leads to new questions, suggesting that there may never be a final understanding of the universe. Engaging with new frontiers in science, technology, or spirituality, like space exploration, quantum physics, or artificial intelligence, may become the next phase of growth. This stage of the journey may also lead to a realization that reaching peak potential is not a final destination but part of a constant evolution.

One with the Universe

Many spiritual traditions such as Buddhism, Hinduism, and Taoism suggest that after self-actualization (or enlightenment), the goal is to dissolve the ego and transcend the notion of individual identity. In this view, the individual merges with the whole, becoming one with the divine or cosmic consciousness.

Are You The Universe?

For instance, Buddhism and Hinduism view self-actualization as attaining liberation from the cycle of birth and rebirth, achieving eternal peace or Nirvana. Bodhisattva traditions in Buddhism emphasize dedicating one's life to helping others reach enlightenment.

Tat tvam asi

Transliteration: "That thou art."

This famous phrase, known as the Mahavakya (Great Saying), signifies that the individual self (Atman) is identical with the ultimate reality, Brahman. It suggests the fundamental unity of all beings with the universe.

In Advaita Vedanta, merging with universal consciousness is part of the cosmic dance (Lila), where creation, destruction, and transformation are endless. These traditions suggest that there is no final point; instead, everything is in flux. It represents the understanding that all individual existence is part of the greater cosmic reality.

A Web of Shared Consciousness

As individuals move through self-actualization, a new horizon opens, one that touches on humanity's collective evolution. This shift raises profound questions about the role of human consciousness in the evolution of society, culture, and the cosmos.

The concept of collective consciousness refers to the idea that individual consciousness is not entirely separate or isolated but is part of a larger, interconnected network of awareness that spans humanity. This notion suggests that our thoughts, emotions, and actions contribute to and are influenced by the collective society's broader mental, emotional, and spiritual states or even the universe. The idea of a web of shared consciousness takes this further by proposing that there is an unseen field or fabric of consciousness that connects all individuals at a fundamental level, much like the internet links computers.

Carl Jung introduced the concept of the collective unconscious, a shared layer of the human psyche containing universal experiences, symbols, and archetypes. According to Jung, the collective unconscious is a repository of all human experiences, and it influences our behavior, dreams, and thoughts. This shared consciousness binds humanity through deep universal themes that transcend individual differences. Similarly, Indian philosophy describes the Akashic Field as a cosmic repository of human knowledge and experience, accessible through deep meditation or mystical experiences. The Akashic Field is relevant to our discussion as it is a concept that supports the idea of a shared field of consciousness. Similarly, in Buddhism, the idea of interconnectedness and dependent origination teaches that all beings are connected through a web of cause and effect. Every action, thought, and emotion influences not only the individual but the entire universe, creating a shared field of consciousness. Enlightened beings like the Bodhisattva are believed to transcend individual awareness and dedicate their lives to helping others reach enlightenment, recognizing that all life is interconnected.

Physicists like Erwin Schrödinger and David Bohm have suggested that consciousness may be a fundamental property of the universe. Bohm's concept of the implicate order proposed that all parts of the universe are interconnected through a deeper underlying reality. In this view, human awareness plays a unique role in the unfolding of the universe's self-awareness.

Are You The Universe?

Philosophers like Teilhard de Chardin have proposed that human consciousness is moving toward an Omega Point, a stage where humanity's collective awareness converges into a higher state of unity and understanding.

If human consciousness contributes to the universe's self-awareness, then humanity's purpose may extend beyond individual goals to shaping reality through intention, creativity, and spiritual insight.

Is There a Final Destination?

The pursuit of self-actualization is not the end but the beginning of a new phase of personal and collective growth. Whether through individual fulfillment, serving a higher purpose, or contributing to humanity's evolution, the journey continues.

Some argue there is no final destination; growth, evolution, and learning continue indefinitely. Even after reaching peak potential or self-actualization, new dimensions of personal and universal exploration open up. Expanding consciousness beyond current human understanding, exploring metaphysical realms or deeper spiritual experiences, and continuously working to improve humanity's future and the planet

Reaching self-actualization often leads to a shift in perspective from focusing on the self to contributing to the greater whole. The journey doesn't stop; it transforms, opening up new dimensions of personal and universal exploration.

The highest potential is not a fixed point but an ongoing process of becoming a dynamic relationship with the self, others, and the universe. The quest to understand and contribute to the broader tapestry of life may indeed be the ultimate purpose for both the individual and humanity as a whole.

References

1. Maslow, A. H. (1969). The Farther Reaches of Human Nature. Viking Press.

2. Jung, C. G. (1969). The Archetypes and the Collective Unconscious. Princeton University Press.

3. Bohm, D. (1980). Wholeness and the Implicate Order. Routledge.

4. Radhakrishnan, S. (1953). The Principal Upanishads. Harper & Row

5. Laszlo, E. (2004). Science and the Akashic Field: An Integral Theory of Everything.

6. Motoyama, H. (1981). Theories of the Chakras: Bridge to Higher Consciousness. Theosophical Publishing House.

7. Laszlo, E. (2006). The Chaos Point: The World at the Crossroads. Hampton Roads Publishing.

Chapter 9

The end of an epic Journey

Throughout this awe-inspiring journey, we've traversed from the primordial vibrations of Om to the expansive realms of consciousness and self-actualization. We have delved into the profound understanding that sound is not just a sensory experience but a fundamental force that shapes the universe and influences our very being.

We began by understanding how sound and vibration are woven into the fabric of the cosmos, influencing the formation of matter and the evolution of life. The Om mantra emerged as a symbolic and literal resonance connecting us to the universe's origins. From there, we turned inward, examining how the human body functions as an electromagnetic field, with energy centers (chakras) that can be aligned and harmonized through practices like meditation, yoga, and sound healing.

Our journey then led us to the flow state, where mind and body align harmoniously, allowing creativity and peak performance to flourish. We explored self-actualization as a personal achievement and a stepping stone toward self-transcendence, where individuals contribute to the greater good and align with universal consciousness. Finally, we embraced the idea of infinite growth, recognizing that the quest to reach our highest potential is an ongoing, ever-evolving process.

The Resonance of Being

Are You The Universe?

At the heart of this journey is the profound recognition of the interconnectedness of all things. Sound, vibration, and consciousness are not isolated phenomena; they are deeply intertwined aspects of existence. By attuning ourselves to the fundamental vibrations of the universe, we tap into a wellspring of potential that transcends the individual self.

This resonance is not just about personal enlightenment; it's about harmonizing with the broader symphony of life. When we align our internal vibrations with those of the universe, we contribute to a collective consciousness that fosters growth, compassion, and unity.

Practical Steps Toward Harmonization

1. Embrace Mindful Practices

- Meditation and Breathwork: Regular meditation helps quiet the mind, making us more attuned to our inner vibrations and the subtle energies around us. Practices like pranayama (controlled breathing) can enhance this connection.

- Yoga and Movement: Engaging in yoga or mindful movement aligns the body's energy centers, promoting physical health and spiritual growth.

2. Harness the Power of Sound

- Chanting and Mantras: Incorporate sound into your daily routine through chanting mantras like Om to align your vibrations with universal frequencies.

Are You The Universe?

- Sound Therapy: Explore sound healing using instruments like singing bowls, tuning forks, or gongs to balance and harmonize your energy field.

3. Cultivate Continuous Growth

- Lifelong Learning: Adopt a growth mindset, embracing new experiences and knowledge as opportunities for expansion.

- Reflective Journaling: Regularly reflect on your thoughts, feelings, and experiences to gain deeper self-awareness and foster personal development.

4. Connect with Nature and the Community

- Nature Immersion: Spend time in natural settings to realign with the Earth's vibrations and rejuvenate your energy.

- Community Engagement: Join communities or group activities that share your interest in personal growth and collective well-being.

Co-Creating a Harmonious Future

As we move forward, the insights gained from understanding the resonance of being can guide us in co-creating a future that embodies harmony, compassion, and collective evolution. By recognizing our role within the larger tapestry of existence, we can promote:

- Empathy and Understanding: Acknowledge the shared vibrations that connect us all, fostering greater empathy toward others.

- Holistic Well-Being: Integrate practices that nurture the mind, body, and spirit, contributing to overall societal health.

The journey toward self-actualization and beyond is a deeply personal yet universally shared experience. By embracing the principles of vibration and resonance, we unlock pathways to profound personal growth and contribute to the elevation of collective consciousness.

An Infinite Quest

Remember that this is an infinite quest, an ongoing process of becoming, learning, and evolving. Each step taken in harmony with the universe amplifies not only our own potential but also the potential of humanity as a whole.

May the resonance of your being echo harmoniously with the universe, guiding you toward ever-expanding horizons of growth, understanding, and fulfillment.

Thank you for embarking on this journey. May the insights and practices explored in this book serve as companions on your path toward realizing your highest potential and contributing to a more harmonious world.